World's
Fastest
Machines

MOTORCYCLES

Charles Hofer

PowerKiDS press.

New York

Published in 2008 by The Rosen Publishing Group, Inc.
29 East 21st Street, New York, NY 10010

First Edition

Editors: Jennifer Way and Nicole Pristash
Book Design: Greg Tucker
Photo Researcher: Nicole Pristash

Photo Credits: Cover, pp. 9, 11, 17, 19, 21 Shutterstock.com; p. 5 © AFP/Getty Images; p. 7, 13 © Getty Images; p. 15 © iStockphoto.com/Sascha Burkard.

Library of Congress Cataloging-in-Publication Data

Hofer, Charles.
  Motorcycles / Charles Hofer. — 1st ed.
      p. cm. — (World's fastest machines)
  Includes index.
  ISBN 978-1-4042-4177-0 (library binding)
  1. Motorcycle racing—Juvenile literature. 2. Motocross—Juvenile literature. I. Title.
  GV1060.H58 2008
  796.75—dc22
                                            2007029177

Manufactured in the United States of America

Contents

Race Day

On race day, thousands of fans come out to the racetrack. The crowd roars for the race to start. Motors rev and tires screech. Riders lean into tight turns just inches (cm) off the ground. With a burst of speed, the riders fly through the straightaways. The bikes kick up dirt. They fly over jumps. It is all part of the cool world of motorcycle racing.

Few sports are as exciting as motorcycle racing. This speed sport mixes machines as fast as rockets with skilled and fearless riders.

Motorcycle racing is a very fun sport. Races, like this one, are great to watch because they are full of action.

Born to Race

In 1885, German **engineer** Gottlieb Daimler tied an engine to a wooden bicycle and the motorcycle was born. By 1903, Americans William S. Harley and Arthur Davidson produced their first motorcycle. Harley-Davidson motorcycles looked cool. They were fast and gave people the freedom to ride the open road. America quickly fell in love with the motorcycle.

Almost as soon as they were invented, people began racing motorcycles. Over the years, motorcycles became faster and more powerful. Soon motorcycles were being built for different types of races.

This is a Harley-Davidson from 1923. The photo was taken at Brooklands racetrack, in England. Brooklands had the first oval racetrack in the world!

The Wild World of Motorcycle Racing

People love racing motorcycles. Some motorcycle races go up steep hills on dirt tracks. Some races feature bikes speeding across snow and ice. Drag bikes are built for high speeds over short tracks.

The two most popular forms of motorcycle racing are road racing and off-road racing. Road racing takes place on **paved** tracks. It can also take place on streets and roads that have been closed off for the race. In these races, sleek speedsters called superbikes are raced. Off-road racing takes place on dirt tracks. This is the world of motocross. In these races, riders test their skills through mud and dirt and over hills and jumps.

Motocross races take place on dirt tracks. Sometimes, special hills are made by hand to make the races harder.

Fast Designs

Superbikes and motocross bikes have two different **designs**. Motocross bikes are fairly large and the rider sits high up in the seat. This design allows for the bike's large **suspension** system. This system lessens the shock of the many jumps and bumps found in motocross tracks.

Superbike riders do not have to worry about jumps and bumps. They are more concerned about speed and control. Superbikes are built low to the ground and are smaller than motocross bikes. This design gives the rider better control. This is very important when taking turns at high speeds.

Superbike races take place in many countries, such as Australia, New Zealand, the United States, and Japan. This superbike race is taking place in Malaysia.

Motocross and Supercross

Off-road racing takes motorcycles to the limit. The most popular type of off-road racing is motocross. In motocross, riders use strong dirt bikes to race over bumpy, unpaved tracks made of dirt, mud, or clay. Motocross tracks often have many sharp twists and turns. Some even have jumps. All these features of the track test the rider's skill. Only the best succeed at motocross.

Supercross is motocross that takes place on an indoor track. Supercross tracks have many jumps. The result is a cool race in which riders put on high-flying shows for the crowd.

Travis Pastrana is one of the best supercross jumpers in the United States. On August 4, 2006, he became the first person ever to land a double backflip in a contest!

Built to Last

The motocross bike is built for speed and strength. During a race, bikes have to move through jumps and bumps, mud, and rocks. These are just a few of the things motocross bikes have to take on while going as fast as possible!

The motocross bike has a special design for riding on bumpy tracks. **Disc brakes** give the rider good control of the bike. These brakes allow the rider to quickly slow the bike to take a tight turn. The motor is built for power. It allows the bike to hit full speed in a straightaway. Tires on a motocross bike have a deep **tread** pattern. This gives the bike better **traction**.

Superbikes

Superbikes are the fastest racing bikes in the world. These colorful bikes have very powerful engines. Unlike motocross, superbike racing takes place on smooth, paved tracks. During races, superbikes regularly go well over 100 miles per hour (161 km/h).

Superbike races take place at lightning speed. Speed records seem to get broken at nearly every race. In the United States, superbike races happen under the American Motorcyclist Association (AMA). The AMA holds wildly popular races in places like Monterey, California, and Daytona, Florida.

Superbikes are made just for racing. You cannot drive them on the streets because they are so fast. This rule is to keep the rider and other drivers safe.

Built for Speed

In superbike racing, it is all about speed. Superbikes have **aerodynamic** designs, which help them go fast. The rider sits low on the bike, tucked behind the windshield. This allows the bike to cut through the air and speed down a track.

Superbike designs are always being changed and tested to make even faster bikes. At places like the Bonneville Salt Flats, in Utah, superbikes break land speed records. In 2004, a superbike reached a record speed of 259.93 miles per hour (418.32 km/h)!

The Fearless Rider

Motocross races require great skill and strength. During races, riders pull off high jumps or dig through sharp turns. They also have to keep from crashing into the other bikes on the track! Motocross riders have to be in top **physical** shape to race. Riders have to be strong enough to control their bike at all times.

Motocross riders have to be well **protected** during races. They wear padding, thick gloves, and strong boots. Superbike riders wear padded jackets and pants. They also wear padded gloves and boots. Most importantly, motocross and superbike riders wear protective helmets at all times.

Motorcycle racers must pay attention to the other drivers when they are racing. Sometimes, they get close enough to touch the other riders!

Into the Future

Motorcycle racing is riding its popularity into the **future**. The X Games is a competition held every year. It features only action sports, including motocross. It was started in 1995. These games help bring in new fans to the world of motocross and other action sports every year. Superbikes are looking to the future, too. More and more races are being held in places like Europe and Asia.

Around the world, people have always had a need for speed. The way things are going, motorcycle racing is showing no signs of slowing down.

Glossary

aerodynamic (er-oh-dy-NA-mik) Made to move through the air easily.

designs (dih-ZYNZ) The plans or the forms of things.

disc brakes (DISK BRAYKS) Brakes on a car or motorcycle, in which the brake pads press against a spinning disc to slow the car or motorcycle.

engineer (en-juh-NEER) A person who uses math and science to design things.

future (FYOO-chur) The time that is coming.

paved (PAYVD) Covered with something hard and human made.

physical (FIH-zih-kul) Having to do with the body.

protected (pruh-TEKT-ed) Kept safe.

suspension (suh-SPENT-shun) A shock-absorbing system in a car or motorcycle.

traction (TRAK-shun) The hold a moving object has on a surface.

tread (TRED) The part of the wheels that touches the ground.

Index

D
Davidson, Arthur, 6
design(s), 10, 14, 18
dirt, 4, 8, 12
disc brakes, 14

E
engine(s), 6, 16

F
fans, 4, 22

G
ground, 4, 10

H
Harley, William S., 6

J
jumps, 4, 8, 10, 12, 14, 20

R
racing, 4, 8, 12, 16, 18, 22
rider(s), 4, 8, 10, 12, 14, 18, 20
road(s), 6, 8
rockets, 4

S
speed(s), 4, 8, 10, 14, 16, 18, 22
sport(s), 4, 22
straightaway(s), 4, 14
superbikes, 10, 16, 18, 22
system, 10

T
tires, 4, 14
traction, 14
turn(s), 4, 10, 12, 14, 20

Web Sites

Due to the changing nature of Internet links, PowerKids Press has developed an online list of Web sites related to the subject of this book. This site is updated regularly. Please use this link to access the list:
www.powerkidslinks.com/wfm/cycle/